NOTES

including
- *Life of the Author*
- *List of Characters*
- *Critical Commentaries*
- *Character Analyses*
- *Review Questions*
- *Selected Bibliography*

by
Lola Amis, M.L.A.
Department of English
Johns Hopkins University

INCORPORATED

LINCOLN, NEBRASKA 68501

Editor	Consulting Editor
Gary Carey, M.A.	*James L. Roberts, Ph.D.*
University of Colorado	*Department of English*
	University of Nebraska

ISBN 0-8220-0874-2
© Copyright 1971
by
Cliffs Notes, Inc.
All Rights Reserved
Printed in U.S.A.

1995 Printing

Cliffs Notes, Inc.   Lincoln, Nebraska

CONTENTS

Native Son Notes

LIFE OF THE AUTHOR

Richard Wright began life on September 4, 1908, in Natchez, Mississippi, on a small farm much in the same manner that his hero, Bigger Thomas, began his life. Deprived, poor, and segregated against, Wright spent much of his early childhood in pain, fear, and shame. His South, like that of Bigger's South, deprived him of a normal childhood. He was continually beaten by his mother and his grandmother for trying to fight back at the segregation imposed upon him. He was also beaten by the whites to whom he had to turn for jobs and he was resentful of the Jim Crow rules by which he had to live. It was with a strong determination, then, that Wright strengthened himself against defeat. He vowed early in his nomadic childhood to leave the South and to go North where blacks were treated like human beings.

Deserted early by an indifferent father, Wright and his brother were left in the care of a sick mother whose weary existence showed in her treatment of her two sons. Wright's autobiography, *Black Boy,* which takes the reader behind the scenes of the first seventeen years of his life in the South, reveals sporadic moves from one town to another, from one job to another, and from one relative to another, always replacing the inconsistencies of his life with other inconsistencies.

At the age of fifteen, Richard Wright wrote his first short story, "The Voodoo of Hell's Half-Acre," for the local newspaper and submitted it in three parts. The story perplexed and frightened his family. His grandmother said that it was a sin to write fiction; being a staunch member of the Seventh-Day Adventist church, her doctrines would not even allow the eating of meat. So, not being able to explain to any member of his family his deep desire to write, Wright dropped the matter for the time but continued to read all the fiction he could find.

Because his family moved from place to place, Richard held a variety of jobs, from porter to post office clerk to grocer to hospital attendant. However, he always kept his major goal in mind: to escape the cruelties of segregation.

It was the Great Depression that drove a large number of blacks toward the North, and, along with them, were Richard Wright, his mother, aunt, and brother. At this time jobs for everyone were hard to find and especially so for Negroes. Richard wandered from job to job with little success of remaining on one job for long. Swallowing his pride, he applied for welfare, or "hand-outs," which consisted of little more than flour, lard, and molasses. However, it was at one of these welfare interviews that Wright met Mrs. Mary Wirth. She took an interest in the young man and helped him get a job in the Federal Negro Theater, a project of the New Deal administration. Bigger's move to Chicago thus finally afforded him the opportunity to fulfill a childhood dream: that of becoming a writer. He had studied at the public library (by having a white man's signature affixed to his library card); he had read such writers as Dreiser, Fitzgerald, Mencken, and Lewis. Now he too had a chance to write. And even though the North crowded him and his race into the Black Belt of Chicago, Richard seized this opportunity to join the Federal Writers' Project in Chicago and to publish two short stories and a poem.

Wright's publications appeared early in the 1930s in several Communist magazines and newspapers. Then, after becoming a member of the Communist party in 1932, Wright was selected to edit one of its party papers. The affiliation with the Communist party eventually led to Wright's meeting famous American writers, as well as European ones. It should perhaps be said that one can easily understand Wright's association with Communist groups: capitalism and racism were enemies of the black man. Negroes in Chicago and other large cities were being encouraged to join the Communist party; it promised something capitalism denied the black man: brotherhood for all. Wright, along with other blacks, succumbed.

In 1937 when Wright was sent to New York to become the editor of the *Daily Worker,* he readily accepted the position. Yet it was this affiliation with the Communist party that has caused many white Americans to shun his publications and to credit him with being just a black man with a loud mouth. Much of the criticism against Richard Wright by his early white critics has stemmed from his being, at one time, a Communist.

Wright, however, did not listen to the critics. He did listen to his new friends and the party, and they encouraged him to continue writing. Thus he began a series of short stories, later published as *Uncle Tom's Children.* Like *Native Son* and *Eight Men,* this first book of Wright's definitively portrays the black man's human condition in white America. All of the characters are, in effect, native sons — products of the white caste ideology. All of them exist in abject conditions of shame, hatred and, most of all, fear. They are treated by the whites as less than human; existence is possible only with excesses of religion, sex, whiskey, or — violence. It was Wright's goal to show to the world that the black man's condition in America could be traced directly to his treatment by the white man.

It was not until January, 1954, that Wright published a volume of political nonfiction. He had, however, been political minded; he had made political speeches all over Europe. This book could easily have been no more than collected speeches, but Wright was never a man to rest on his laurels. He aimed this new volume at Africa; it concerned Ghana and the abject conditions of the black people and their treatment by the British. Wright struggled over a title for this huge volume of material and finally decided upon *Black Power.* Many readers today, of course, do not realize that it was Wright himself who first used the term which has now become known in many other contexts. Unfortunately, *Black Power* was not received well on either side of the ocean. Like Harriet Beecher Stowe's *Uncle Tom's Cabin,* the book was either banned in toto or whole sections of it deleted.

Among Wright's later books are *The Outsider* (1953) and *Savage Holiday* (1954). Cross Damon is a black man struggling

to survive in *The Outsider;* Erskine Fowler is a white man
struggling to survive in *Savage Holiday*. Yet both men are part
of the long line of Wright's characters who search for a desire to
live—despite their hostile environment, despite a world that
rejects every effort toward self-realization. In his later years, it
was Wright's most driving desire to show the plight of not only
black men, but of *all* oppressed men, everywhere. As he grew
older, he moved from the theme of the black man's debasement
and the black man's struggle for happiness to every man's
struggle. In *The Outsider,* for instance, the reader is not constantly reminded that Cross Damon is a black man; rather, he seems
to be the embodiment of all men, men both black and white,
both American and European, Asian and African.

LIST OF CHARACTERS

Bigger Thomas

A young Negro, twenty years old; vicious, vile and mean; he
hates himself and all human society, especially that part
of society which made him into a monster.

Buddy Thomas

Bigger's brother; he accepts the standards set for him by the
white society against which Bigger rebels.

Vera Thomas

Bigger's sister; she is timid and afraid, almost afraid of her
own shadow.

Mrs. Thomas

Bigger's mother; tired and worn out from the daily task of
living in abject poverty, persecution and pain, she cannot understand Bigger. She prods him daily into further differences between them, especially by continually predicting Bigger's fate.

Mr. Dalton

A white businessman who owns the rat-infested hovels in which blacks must live; yet he gives large sums of money to the NAACP and to other charitable organizations for the "uplifting" of the blacks, who are, ironically, oppressed by this man's very existence.

Mrs. Dalton

Physically blind, as well as psychologically blind, she is unable to see that her charitable gestures, like those of her husband, are not wanted and are not appreciated by the black society that wants what the white society seems to have: equality, dignity, and financial security.

Mary Dalton

The immature daughter of the Daltons; rich and spoiled like her mother, she is psychologically blind. She treats Bigger like a test case for both her own white-caste ideology, concerning the Negro, and for the Communist party and its ideology. She is in love with Jan Erlone, a Communist.

Jan Erlone

A Communist; Mary Dalton's lover. He joins Mary in patronizing Bigger, the black outsider.

Peggy

The Daltons' housekeeper; she thinks the Daltons are good Christian people because they give money to Negro charities.

Bessie Mears

Bigger's black girl friend who, like Bigger, is caught in a web of socio-economic frustrations within white-oriented society.

Buckley

State prosecutor.

Boris A. Max.

Bigger's lawyer.

Gus, G. H., and Jack

Bigger's hoodlum friends.

Doc

Owner of the poolroom, the hangout for Bigger and his friends.

CRITICAL COMMENTARIES

BOOK I
FEAR

Ralph Ellison declares in *Shadow and Act* that in Richard Wright's fiction, the Negro has a choice of one of three roles to assume: he can assume the role of passivity designed for him by the southern whites and resolve his personal conflicts through the emotional catharsis of religion; or he can strive for and establish his own middle-class society and thereby consciously or unconsciously become the white man's accomplice in oppression; or he can reject the entire southern white ideology and assume the role of a criminal, which will inevitably erupt into physical violence. In *Native Son*, Bigger Thomas chooses the latter.

Bigger is an embodiment of the black revolt against the injustices of the white caste system, and his revolt takes the form of crime against the white society. Born into a society that is white, hostile, and indifferent, Bigger becomes the total embodiment of that society's hatreds, prejudices, and resentments against the black man. Bigger is filled with hatred, shame, frustration, and resentment against himself first, his family, his friends, and, of course, against the white world that keeps him an outsider. Bigger becomes a man without a conscience, a man without hope, or love, or religion; he becomes a man without a home, without family, or even friends. In other words, Bigger becomes "no man."

The opening scene of the novel sets the tone for the entire work; the scene is a one-room, rat-infested apartment where an alarm clock is ringing loudly. The author chooses the sound imagery, the ringing of the clock, as his first major motif; it has a jarring, electrifying effect on the reader. The clanging of the clock signals a warning; it is like a cry of death, symbolic of both literal and figurative time passing in Bigger's life. This time (or death) motif is repeated many times in the novel and is both physically, as well as emotionally, significant to Bigger. Mrs. Thomas yells for Bigger to turn off the clock and turn on the light. Bigger would rather stay in his world of dreams. Light will reveal the poverty and squalor around him; darkness will hide it. Bigger would rather blot out reality. Later, however, we will see that Bigger must acknowledge time — and reality — and, with the passing of time, both Bigger and his mother will have to face death — Bigger, his own; Mrs. Thomas, her son's.

Indeed, one of the major problems posed by this novel concerns death, specifically murder. Bigger, for example, has no father; he has only memories of his father's being murdered in a racial incident in the South. He has no physical father to belong to and he has no country to which he truly belongs. The parallel is striking. Bigger's "home" is really no home. The ghetto where he lives is a world of bleakness, of poverty, of privation, surrounded by a white society which keeps blacks always on the outside. So we get to the subtleties of murder — in how many ways has the white man "murdered" the black man? And who is ultimately responsible for retaliation? The white world is denying Bigger life; it is caging him in a ghetto. Bigger is living like a criminal, yet he has committed no crime — except that he is a black man; for that, he is sentenced to a filthy existence in the black prison of the ghetto.

In contrast to this black world is the masters' world—the white world—where there is plenty of food, privacy, and comfort. It is a sensuous world of easy love and liquor and mattresses stuffed with dollars. It is a world of smart, privileged people. Bigger is naturally curious about the white world, this world that he cannot wholly believe exists, for he has never seen it, except at the movies. It is a fantasy world filled with everything Bigger's world lacks. In fact, it often seems as though it were an illusion. And because Bigger is not allowed to enter this world, he becomes hostile. He is filled with shame because the white man makes him feel that he is not an equal; he is filled with fear because the white man is ready to kill him for no reason except that he's a "nigger." Finally he is filled with violence, especially violence, toward that society that represses his chance of becoming a man.

It is with an act of violence, then, that Wright opens his novel. Bigger kills a fat, vicious rat that literally threatens his family's existence. But we realize that, like the rat which he kills, Bigger is also mean, vicious, and vindictive; he enjoys brutalizing others, especially those of his own race who are too weak or timid to strike back at him or at the white man. His need to brutalize others is his way of reacting against his own brutalization. But, like the rat he kills, Bigger will in turn be killed because the white world will fear him. They will fear Bigger and hate him as thoroughly as Bigger hates and fears the rat.

As Bigger wanders aimlessly around the streets of the ghetto, Wright emphasizes the limited choices in life which blacks have. Whites not only have millions of choices at jobs but at everything else they want in life. But Bigger, being black, has always been hindered from developing himself. His remark that he could fly a plane if he had a chance evokes laughter from Gus. Yet Gus agrees: *if* Bigger were not black, *if* Bigger had money, *if* they (the whites) let him go to aviation school, Bigger could fly a plane. Gus repeatedly uses the word "if" and emphasizes "black" and "money" and "white," suggesting that in addition to the whites' segregation of the blacks, the white man controls America's money, a capitalistic advantage which the blacks do not have.

Having no money, having no chance to get a good job, having to face the shame of always being an outsider, Bigger naturally turns to one of the few ways blacks have of getting easy money: crime. But note that in Bigger's code, even in his code of violence, there are certain taboos. He entertains the idea of robbing Blum's store, but his stomach tightens, he becomes hot all over, and he feels ready to snap. He knows that he can never rob a white man; this would be a violation of the ultimate taboo. This is another illusion of Bigger's; he is dreaming of something he will never do. He cannot enter the white man's world — even to rob him.

On the other hand, it is easy to think about robbing blacks, even doing it, because white policemen never really try to solve crimes against blacks. The white policeman turns his head indifferently to what is happening in the black neighborhood. Only when a black man strikes out at a white man is there any official police concern. Bigger hates this double standard, but he is ultimately frightened of it, hence the title of this section of the novel, "Fear."

In this first section, note particularly how Wright introduces the symbols, images, and motifs that serve to give structure as well as credence to the story. The major motif of the novel is fear, and all the other symbols and images are dependent upon fear — fear in the abstract and fear as a physical presence. It underlies virtually every action of the novel and motivates Bigger's crimes. Fear and hatred, facets of the same emotion, are Bigger's only feelings when he is faced, literally, with the white world. Bigger always envies the white world from a distance, but when he has to face it, envy is quickly displaced by waves of fear.

This feeling of Bigger's must be understood in order to understand the novel. It is a fear, almost inborn, which has been reinforced by the actions of whites for as long as Bigger can remember. It is not, from Bigger's viewpoint, an unreasoning fear; it is, however, an overwhelming emotion that leaves him helpless in its grip. He is literally possessed by fear in the sense that persons once were possessed by the devil. Although Wright makes it quite clear that the whites in the novel are not wholly what Bigger thinks they are, he also makes it clear that Bigger is incapacitated by fear of the whites to the point where he cannot make judgments of their actions, nor can he rationally determine what his own actions should be. The result of this paralyzing, irrational fear is the plot of the novel.

Supporting the main motif are numerous symbols and images. Heat and cold convey the extent of Bigger's fear; he sweats in terror and he turns burning hot; he is cold in the abandoned building and freezing on the roof by the water tank. His hatred is symbolized as being like a "red-hot iron." He feels, he says, as though someone were poking a red-hot iron down his throat.

Light and dark images are frequent. Bigger fears the unending darkness of Mrs. Dalton's blindness, he is afraid of the dark trap of Mary's bedroom, and he hates what whites have made of his dark skin. Yet he welcomes the safe darkness of the basement that can hide so much. The light and dark motifs are ambivalent and complex. On the one hand, Bigger hates what whites have made of his dark skin; he is conditioned to see his blackness as a negative darkness. He hates the darkness of Mary's bedroom and Mrs. Dalton's blindness; this is the darkness of the white enemy. Bigger, however, loves darkness when it offers protection from what whites have caused: the poverty of Bigger's home and community. He welcomes the darkness of the basement because he is separated from the whites upstairs; the only white in the basement is dead. Yet even here his security is threatened by the presence of the white cat.

In addition to Wright's imagery, note the name he gives to his main character: Bigger. Is Bigger big? Is he a big man? Who is he "bigger" than? The answer, we discover, is that Bigger is a scared, weak man in Book I. He is afraid and he has to prove himself, even in the black world. In the poolroom, Gus becomes his scapegoat, his hate-object. He calls Gus a coward, but it is Bigger who is the real coward. He makes Gus lick the blade of the knife, but Bigger is not a big man by doing this; he is living in a dream world, trying to enhance his self-esteem. The white world will not let Bigger become a man so this is the way that Bigger tries to be "big" and be a man. By calling his hero "Bigger," Wright makes us aware of Bigger's sense of inferiority. But we do not condemn Bigger for brutalizing Gus. We understand; he is trying to hide his feelings of shame and inadequacy, a shame and fear so great as to emasculate his very existence were he to acknowledge it.

One of the ways Bigger escapes from shame and fear is by going to the movies where he can sit and dream and wonder at the glamour of his oppressor's world. He can see lush golf greens, dancing parties, happy whites, and *money* everywhere. Bigger sees all these things in "The Gay Woman" and, by chance, he sees something else: a Communist. Bigger doesn't know what a Communist is, but he does see the Communist as the movie's villain, a wild, crazy bomb thrower. Later, two Communists, Max and Jan, will attempt to befriend Bigger; while other whites will cry for blood, a Communist will be pleading for Bigger's life in the name of reason and humanity. But, as we soon realize, Max's reasoning will have little effect when matched with the white world's passionate fear and hatred of Bigger.

It is, in fact, because of the movie that Bigger decides to try and make a wedge for himself into the rich, tempting white world. But it is so foreign and so frightening a world that Bigger does not go alone. He enters the white world, but not before returning home to get his gun and knife. For he enters the white world as an underling, as a servant, as a chauffeur. In short, Bigger will be hired to do what the white man is too lazy to do—drive his own car. It is only because he takes his weapons with him that Bigger is able to feel equal to the white man. Yet he has not even met the white boss-man yet. And, as he nears the Dalton home, he is very aware of the laws and customs and mores that separate men because of the color of their skin. He realizes that blacks cannot go where they want to; cats can, but blacks can't. Blacks are condemned to a small area on Chicago's South Side.

Waiting for the door to open to the Dalton home, Bigger is plagued by a death vision, and we recall Mrs. Thomas' prediction in the novel's opening scene: "You'll regret how you living some day." Again Wright brings in allusions to fire and heat, images very important to the murder later in the novel. Bigger still burns with hate and pain in the presence of a white man — despite the fact that he has brought his weapons. He has attempted to be a man, to be equal, but something inside him, something he doesn't understand, won't let him be a man. The white man has done a thorough job through the centuries: he has convinced the black man that he is not as good as the white man, that he should play "nigger" and "boy" when he is in the presence of a white man. And Bigger acts this role on cue. He shuffles his feet, his shoulders are sloped, and his head is bowed. Like a dog, he licks his lips and, like an ape, he scratches his head. No one told Bigger to act this way; this is a poison that the white man has put into the very psyche of the black man. It is something understood and expected. The white man has given the blacks this role ever since they brought them from Africa. Then, the heavy chains around their necks and on their wrists and ankles made them stoop and shuffle; they came from Africa and the weight of their slave chains made them look, to the white man's eyes, like apes. And, in order to justify kidnapping and enslaving blacks, the white master convinced himself that they were not human. Thus, to the white man, blacks have been apes ever since. Look at Bigger, standing before Mr. Dalton: his knees are slightly bent, his lips partly open, and his shoulders stooped. This is the image of an ape. Wright shows us how conditioned, subconsciously, Bigger is to play the "nigger" role, only because of the perennial assertion by the white world that all blacks are shiftless and lazy, actually a "little lower than the brutal beasts." Not only does the white community, both rich and poor alike, believe this but they have convinced some Negroes of their own abject condition, of their own personal worthlessness. This attempt at conditioning has made it necessary for black Americans to fight against this conditioning.

In the Dalton home, Wright once more brings in the time motif, as well as the light motif. Bigger encounters a clock ticking somewhere behind him as he is being interviewed by Mr. Dalton. He suddenly has an impulse to look at it. This subconscious desire to look at time is symbolic, of course, of his impending crime against the Dalton household and his unconscious fear that something horrendous is going to happen to him. Many times a clock in this novel will seem to warn Bigger of approaching danger. The clock-time-death motif was used, for instance, when Bigger walked toward Doc's place to keep his appointment with his friends. The clock was a warning then that he had twelve minutes to invent an excuse to keep him from participating in a robbery of which he was afraid. Later, as he neared the Dalton home, a clock boomed five times, loudly warning him not to go near the Dalton house. Finally, after he has committed the murder of Mary Dalton, he will hear a clock; but instead of booming, as it did earlier when he neared the Dalton house, it will be ticking now. It warns no longer; now it is merely a clock, ticking away Bigger's time.

As mentioned earlier, Wright has used the idea of light and reality since the novel's beginning. In bed, Bigger was content to leave the light off, not to face the light. Note that leaving his house for the Dalton home, the light is dying over the rooftops in the western sky; the street lights come on, but the sky is black. It is a dark omen as Bigger approaches the Dalton home.

Inside the Dalton home, the house of the white man, there are various kinds of light. Using the dim light of the lamps (illusionary light), Wright is suggesting a symbol of the psychological blindness of the entire Dalton household. Note that even the housekeeper addresses Bigger as though she were superior to him: "Are you the Thomas boy?" Bigger is twenty years old; he is no boy. Yet to the white world, a black man is always a "boy." Even white servants feel infinitely superior to black servants.

The Daltons are white people and they think they are friends of the black man, but they are blind to the reality of their situation and the situation of the blacks. Indeed, Mrs. Dalton is physically blind; she is a symbol of the white society that believes itself to be liberal and a friend to the blacks. Her white skin, her white hair, and her white cat are a parody of good and innocence. She speaks to her husband of "injecting" Bigger "into his new environment," as though he were an animal in a scientific experiment. The Daltons pride themselves on having a "deep interest in colored people." They give money, millions of dollars, to the "colored people," but they give it in terms of ping-pong tables. It is awesome to imagine such an empty gesture. The Daltons are the major owners of Bigger's ghetto; they keep it run-down, rat-infested, and black. Yet they extend their "Christian" hands to the blacks with presents of ping-pong tables. The white man gives the black man ping-pong tables because the black man is supposed to play games, like a "boy," and forget about four people — two women and two men — living cramped in a one-room hole on the South Side. This act of generosity, this fraud, makes the white man feel good and magnanimous; it whitewashes his prejudice. His white skin is a symbol of sham innocence and goodness, as is the excess of "whiteness" in the Dalton household. The Daltons believe that they know about the black world. They are ignorant, however; the Daltons know only the blacks who are content to play "nigger" for them.

Mary Dalton enters and the reader should note here that Bigger's hatred for her stems from the black man's inherent fear of white women, or rather what white men have taught black men to fear: there must never be any type of social or sexual intercourse between black men and white women. This factor has become an integral part of the black man's soul. Sex is often the root of many problems in the black-white relationship because white men have felt free to have sexual intercourse with black women, but a black man must *never* touch a white woman. This is the white man's law, and many a Negro has been lynched or castrated because he so much as smiled at a white woman. In Book III, for example, note that the prosecuting attorney, as well as the entire white community, insists that Bigger raped

Mary Dalton before murdering her. It is inconceivable to the white man that the contrary is true, that Bigger did not molest Mary sexually and that her death was, in fact, accidental.

Knowing this without thinking about the white-black double standard, Bigger recoils from any type of relationship with Mary Dalton. Irony here presents itself again, for the reader knows about these double standards and realizes Bigger's fears, while Mary Dalton seems completely oblivious to rules of any kind.

With Jan Erlone, Bigger feels this same sense of fear and frustration. He shrinks from Jan's handshake and is overwhelmed with panic when Jan insists upon being called "Jan" instead of "Mr. Erlone." In Bigger's code, a white man does not really accept a black man as an equal; Jan and Mary do not belong to his world, nor he to theirs. These white people are a part of the white world of terror; they belong to the system which functions to restrict blacks from socializing with whites. Shaking Jan's hand, eating in the same restaurant with Jan and Mary, even though the restaurant is black, sitting next to them in the same car, touching, calling a white man by his first name are social forms which are alien to Bigger. No wonder he feels naked and lost. A black man cannot easily accept a white man as a friend. They are his enemies; he has been taught it and he has seen its effects. The white man has created an enemy and he has the luxury, if he deigns, to be kind, occasionally, to that enemy. But what Jan does not realize is that his "friendly" acts are not enough for Bigger to see him as being any different from other whites.

During the ride along the lake front, Bigger can only half-listen to the white voices; he recoils from talk of the "revolution" and the idea of blacks with whites. He cannot answer their questions pertaining to the Communistic dogma of overthrowing the government. Such terminology means nothing to him, a black man from Chicago's South Side. As when he killed the rat, Bigger wants to leap at Mary and destroy her soft voice with her "daring" suggestion that they visit one of those "colored places" that serve good food. She wants to sample some soul food; she wants to go slumming and see "life" and be friends with the blacks—for a few hours—before she goes back to playing the avant-garde, rich white liberal. Bigger does not understand himself, but he does know that he would like to claw at Mary, to get rid of her interest in "his" people. He knows that to her, blacks are not *really* people, but a lesser, curiosity-level of human beings. At one point Mary says of blacks: "Yet they *must* live like we live. They're *human*." Human, to her, means having a car, good food, freedom, money, and happiness. She has no idea of the black experience; no white man can. Eating black-cooked food and trying to sing "Swing Low, Sweet Chariot," is experiencing blackness to Mary. It's a game that she doesn't even realize she's playing. She tries to be a "bit" black and also a white *grande dame* at the same time. While they are eating, for example, Mary reminds Bigger that her small trunk has to be taken down to the station and tells him when to pick it up. She'll be a "soul sister" but only as long as she can keep giving orders to her "black brother."

What Mary and Jan do not know is that Bigger's black world is a black hell. They aren't seeing the black world at all. They are only making Bigger feel worthless. They think that together they can achieve the "revolution" and that Bigger will then become "a real American." The situation would be ludicrous were it not so painful.

Dazed by the experience and by the soft heat of the rum, Bigger listens, half in a dream, to the drone of Mary and Jan's revolutionary ideas. The effect of the rum gives him a strange sense of "bigness," of "equality," with the whites. Though not drunk, Bigger is high, and the alcohol gives him a sense of power. The alcohol also does things to Mary. It makes her unaware of what she is doing, such as laying her head on Bigger's shoulder and arousing his sexual impulses, already stimulated by the rum.

As far as we know, Bigger has never touched a white woman before; he has seen their bodies only in the movies. Now, carrying Mary to her room, he has a white woman in his arms. This unreal world of the whites is *real*—and in his arms. This is reality, yet it is the most unreal situation Bigger has ever encountered: to be suddenly working for a white family, then to have their daughter in his arms, in her bedroom. It was probably fantastic to a black man from the ghetto in the 40s. Likewise fantastic is the appearance of Mrs. Dalton. She is ghost-like as she floats to Mary's bed. Bigger is terrified that she can sense his presence in the room. His first impulse is to bolt from the room, but he stays —frozen by the white, blind presence.

Functioning as a central intelligence, Wright makes it clear to us that it is beyond Mrs. Dalton's comprehension to know, or even sense, that Bigger is in the room. Not only is she physically blind but she is also psychologically blind. Even though she gives large sums of money to black charity, she is not aware of their real world; likewise she is not aware that Bigger is in the room. Such a thought is impossible for her. Shut up as she has been all her life, in her own private, white world of choices and her white caste ideology (concerning the blacks), it is inconceivable that a black man could be in her white daughter's bedroom at two o'clock in the morning. It is this—the white man's total ignorance of blacks as living, breathing, pulsating beings—that gives birth to men like Bigger Thomas.

Why does Bigger murder Mary Dalton? Because Mrs. Dalton "floats" toward him, like a ghostly, deadly essence from the white world, and Bigger, out of fear of losing his job, out of hatred for this white girl who has tried to toy with the black experience, out of shame of his being found here, presses the pillow too long and too hard and too deeply into Mary's struggling face. Bigger murders because of fear (the title of this section of the novel), fear of the white man, fear so overwhelming and so all-consuming that it turns a man into a monster. Bigger kills because he is afraid of being discovered; after all, he is a black in the room of a girl who is white. Stifled by years of privation and segregation in his private black hell; he is unable to act rationally. A white man *could* run; a white man *could* be caught; a white man *could* explain his presence. But a black man does not have these choices. He is unable to respond as a normal human being. So, like a cornered beast, Bigger must protect himself, even if he must commit murder. He commits an act which even he himself is unaware that he is capable of doing. Abandoned now by all sense of logic, he knows that he must act, act alone, according to the laws of instinct. He is responsible to no man, to no God, to no group or race. He alone must become the creator of his actions, of his own consequences.

As he prepares to dispose of Mary's body, he is surrounded by the roar of the fire in the furnace, the coals burning red, and the fire blazing and quivering. The author repeatedly refers to the color red. Bigger is going to burn Mary, a shocking climax to the murder, but consider how well it suggests what the white man has figuratively done to Bigger. Bigger burns with hate and with shame because he is a black man. But the white man is responsible for Bigger's inner hell. And Bigger is burning one member of the white society who has made him burn with fury and frustration. This is not a conscious act of retaliation, but it is retaliation. It is grotesque, but it is perhaps a kind of violent justice.

Yet even more horrifying than the idea of burning Mary's body is the fact that Bigger will have to cut off her head in order to fit the body in the furnace. Yet isn't this what the white man has done to the black man for generations? He has, figuratively, decapitated him, refused to recognize his mind, his creativity, his worth; he has made him faceless and dumped him into a stereotype mold of being less than human—a headless, faceless nobody. The horror of the bloody head lying on the newspaper beneath the furnace is shocking to read, but the butchering of the black man's psyche—his head, heart, genitals, and soul—is ultimately more terrifying. Bigger is physically, brutally, gruesomely murdering a white girl; but her parents, and she herself, slowly and painfully, have tortured the life out of many blacks—in the name of "Negro charity."

At the end of Book I, after Bigger has murdered Mary Dalton and is leaving to return home for the night, it is important to notice that there are no clocks to "boom" or to warn Bigger of impending danger. All is quiet as he slips into his place in the one-room, rat-infested apartment beside his brother. There is only the idea of sleep. Just as a clock opened the novel, so the quiet of sleep closes this first section. Bigger is able to sleep quickly because he has killed. To understand this, we must remember that earlier in the day Bigger's fear of whites prevented him from robbing, but now at the end of the day he has murdered one of those he feared. He is relieved and he can sleep. Yet, on another level, his sleeping here is more than merely sleeping; symbolically, the Bigger of this section is dead at the end of Book I.

BOOK II
FLIGHT

At the beginning of Book II, here again are Wright's sleep-awake motifs that began and ended Book I. For instance, no sooner does Bigger close his eyes than they snap open. But unlike the sleep-awake motif in Book I, which was concerned with an actual light switch, this time Bigger becomes aware of time as though an electric switch were being turned on in his brain. Instead of being awakened, as he was in Book I by the strident clanging of an alarm clock, the reference now is to an electric switch; thus, this can be seen as a symbol of foreboding, or as an unconscious reference to the electric chair, where Bigger will die. As Bigger was psychologically, as well as emotionally, dead at the end of Book I, here is a primitive sensing of his physical death in the electric chair.

Tied in a knot of impulses, Bigger struggles to become awake and to face the reality of what he has done. In Book I, Bigger tried *not* to think; he tried to avoid awakening. Now he tries to grasp the fact that he has actually killed a white woman. His conscious mind denies the murder, but his subconscious mind struggles to face the truth. He is in a room filled with deep sleep, as Wright says, suggesting death images; Bigger has killed, has fled, yet here is his family, lying sleeping around him. They lie as if under a death spell. He is unable to fully comprehend this new day, this new present, in a room filled with silence and sleep. The room is real; there is snow falling outside, but Bigger's conscious mind refuses to acknowledge these images of reality. Again he is caught between illusion and reality, between life and death, between existing in a vacuum and existing in a world that still keeps him on the outside.

Then Wright recounts the murder. It happened so quickly, during only the last few pages of Book I that we, and Bigger, must review and recall the murder of Mary Dalton. The horror of Bigger's sudden violence is emphasized: how he smothered her, cut off her head, and stuffed her body in the blazing furnace. We, like Bigger, must realize how unreal this past must seem, juxtaposed to a quiet, sleeping family and silent snow falling outside. Bigger has killed. He, who was afraid to rob a white man, has murdered a white girl and hacked off her head. There were hints, of course, that Bigger was violent—the slashing of the pool table, his ordering Gus to lick the knife blade—but the murder happened without warning. Then it was over and Bigger was asleep. The sudden bloody climax to Book I left us stunned. Likewise, this morning Bigger is stunned. He is not the same person he was yesterday.

When Bigger's family finally awakens, notice that he looks about himself guiltily to see if his family notices anything different; he wonders if he is acting strangely. One should remember, though, that Bigger has "acted" all his life; in Book I, Wright told us that Bigger hid himself behind "an attitude of iron reserve," behind a wall. He acted tough to protect the confused, frightened Bigger that no one knew. Now, he must strengthen this wall; he *must* "act." And he must act, not to protect a secret self, but to protect his very life. He must act with his family, with the Daltons, with the private detective, Britten, and with the reporters. Now his acting is his only chance of survival; this is irony, really, for acting heretofore was considered his only means for survival. Now, however, the acting is desperate. And, besides the nervous anxiety about acting, Bigger has an added problem: the temptation to tell. The knowledge that *he* has committed a murder—against the enemy—bolsters his self-esteem. If he "acts," he saves his life; yet if he tells what he has done, he is a black champion. A new kind of anxious excitement thrills him as he reviews the events of the past few hours. Knowing on the one hand that he must be on his guard against revealing what he has done, he wants to shout his accomplishment to the world. From being a "no man" in Book I, Bigger has become a *man* to himself.

He watches his family as they go about their daily habits of getting dressed, eating breakfast, and preparing for work. He smirks secretly at their insignificance, compared to his new importance; he even begins to consider the murder as deliberate. Now he thinks he committed it on purpose; we know, however, that it was an accident; Bigger did not commit premeditated murder. Nevertheless, he begins to convince himself of a growing importance as he mentally views everyone around him as being blind and himself as being the only one who can "see" things as they really are.

When Bigger meets his friends at Doc's place, he is convinced that they too are blind, blind to his rebirth and resurrection from the black world of fear. He has killed one of the "white blur." He feels now that he is no longer conditioned by what people think of him. He no longer has to despair at being nobody in a world filled with white somebodys. Drunken now with the power of creation, Bigger is no longer a mere "nigger." For the first time he is master of his fate; he is a *man*. No one can frighten him now. He renews his strength by thinking about having killed a white heiress from the world of the white blur; in effect, he becomes his own god in a godless existence. He creates his own image where there was none before – save for the image given him by white society as a stereotyped, black, "no-good nigger."

Thus the death of Mary becomes Bigger's rebirth and resurrection. He is born out of the death of Mary of the white world. Bigger Thomas re-creates himself in a way that is the exact reverse of the Christ story. Christ was created from the virgin Mary; Bigger was created from the death of (probably) a white virgin. In playing God, Bigger makes himself God. And while pretending to become stronger than the force that has always kept him a part of the black background, Bigger becomes a super-man. For even though negative as his status might be, somehow he has become a person to be reckoned with. He is a kind of black anti-Christ.

Bigger wants to stand up and shout his deed to the universe. He wishes to become an image in everybody's mind, an image of a-murderer-of-a-white-girl so that he can win for himself admiration, if not approval, in the eyes of the world. Bigger is no longer just another black; he is new; he has done away with one of the whites that tried to play God to the blacks; now he is playing God to the white world.

Bigger's unconscious mind, which according to Freudian psychology is the seat of suppressed emotions and undesirable social mores suddenly emerges from the darkness of the id and springs into fruition. Bigger thrills to the knowledge that he has accomplished a unique kind of miracle. As he boards the bus to the Daltons' house, he wants to stand up and shout to the world his great feat. These all-powerful urges almost overcome his better judgment. He must be on guard at all times from this type of rashness which might lead to his exposure. At least one part of his new self-concept still realizes the dangers of exposure. Thus Bigger merely sits, acting humble, as if he were still the subservient "nigger" of yesterday.

It is interesting to watch Bigger's relationship with Britten, the white private detective hired by Mr. Dalton to solve the disappearance of his daughter. In a rather shrewd cat-and-mouse game, similar to that played by Raskolnikov in Dostoevsky's *Crime and Punishment,* Bigger dodges from one set of questions and from one set of circumstances to another. Yet he is never really trapped by Britten's hard-core interrogation. Bigger's alibi is so well planned and so well rehearsed that no one forces him to confess either to the disappearance or to the murder of Mary Dalton. It is in these repeated cross-examinations and interrogations between Bigger and Britten that one sees a new and different picture of Bigger. The "nigger" Bigger becomes someone very sharp, someone who can secretly and sadistically manipulate the white detective and the white reporters to his own advantage. With all of Britten's skill and power in tracking down "nigger-criminals," he never really breaks through Bigger's alibi.

Again it is interesting to note that the white world finds it hard to believe that a "nigger" could have planned and manipulated the ransom note idea. Yet it is easy for them to conceive that the idea was born in the brain of a white man, Jan Erlone, whom Bigger implicates as the murderer. It is even harder for this same white world to conceive that a black man could murder a white woman or kill her accidentally without first having sexually molested her. To the white society that has always set the mores and standards for the black man to follow, the black man and rape are synonymous. Therefore, it was immediately understood that Bigger had raped Mary when the reporters discovered her bones in the furnace. It is by pure chance, then, that Bigger is caught and connected with the murder of Mary Dalton. This point must be made clear to the reader in order for the reader to understand fully why Bigger kills Bessie, why Bigger never repents of his crime, why he does not hold himself responsible, and why, in the end, the reader too must exonerate Bigger, if unwillingly. A later discussion of this point will be made in Max's defense of Bigger at his trial.

Concerning Bigger's relationship with Bessie, we realize that basic love is absent from Bigger's world. In a world which has never given him love, he gives none back in return. He tolerates a nagging mother, a timid sister, and a complacent brother; he uses a frustrated Bessie, his fatalistic and drunken girlfriend, to gratify his sensual lusts, and he regards Mary Dalton as a part of the white world which has no real value. He neither recognizes nor accepts the individuality of any other person. But, on the other hand, the white world has never recognized the individuality of the black man.

Love, then, is not an ingredient, nor is human compassion a part, of Bigger's character. He is alone — always outside the world — always, he lives in terms of himself versus the outside world.

He continually hides behind his wall, venturing forth only those times when he is forced to face his fears—fears of being captured or punished by the same social structure from whence he fled.

Further, in his relationship with Bessie, Bigger conceals his own ineptness and weaknesses by blaming others for any failure he has encountered. He blames Bessie in exactly the same way that he blames Mary; each is responsible for her own murder. After all, wasn't it Mary's fault that he had to smother her with a pillow when she came home drunk after making him eat and drink with her when he didn't want to? And wasn't it Bessie who kept nagging him to tell her of his scheme? If both girls had left him alone, neither girl would have been murdered. To Bigger, it isn't his fault that they are dead. In killing them, he was just acting as an agent. They stepped out of line, so he executed them. In rationalizing his life's situation, Bigger kills reality. And, once this metaphysical murder is achieved, he proceeds to re-create a new reality and new esteem for himself. These murders prove one thing: Bigger can be a man to himself. In all his life the two murders—of Bessie and Mary—are the most meaningful things that have ever happened to Bigger Thomas.

Bigger's flight takes place in the Black Belt of Chicago's South Side within a radius of thirty-five blocks, from 18th Street to 53rd Street. This scene is written rather differently now; Wright speaks of Bigger in concrete terms, rather than in abstract images, depicting his every action as an action of a soul lost in fear, shame, and hatred. Everywhere, in every scene, there is conflict, tension, and terror: terror of friends, terror of society itself but, most of all, terror of "self."

Because the very essence of Bigger's life is a struggle for self-realization, self-association with the outside world, Bigger's plight is a plight of futility in the worlds of black and white—to neither of which he belongs. He cannot now belong to the black world because the black world is also a place of self-denial; it is a world where blacks *ought* to join together, but instead it is a place where blacks shout that Bigger's murder will result in many blacks being killed.

In a similar way, the white world also shuts Bigger out. He has invaded it, has killed off one small corner; this is the world of his dream-conquest, but it is immense and powerful; not only does it shut Bigger out, but it pursues him. And, caught now like the rat in the novel's opening scene, Bigger must try to escape. He must try to escape into the rat hole of the black world. The Black Belt is literally that; it is a twisting, tightening entanglement of empty buildings and empty lives; it is a place of dark fear and shame and hate. It is with repugnance that Bigger remembers this world. His mother with her way of singing about religion and Christ and love; Bessie, always crying the Blues about working hard and getting nothing out of life but a cheap drink of whiskey; and his brother, Buddy, who is content with living his life without a fight—all these, to Bigger, are blind— blind to what really matters in life. The only thing Bigger has left in this black world is his gun—not a person he can trust— only a gun. The gun is a symbol of Bigger's manhood, his only real weapon against both worlds, the black and the white.

Pursued by over eight thousand white men in a house-to-house search of over one thousand black homes, and armed with rifles, tear gas, flashlights, and photos of the killer, these white men terrorize the black people into a frenzy of horrendous fear. No one is spared the shame of the search: men, women, and children alike are awakened in the middle of the night with searchlights and guns.

Each news account of the Dalton murder accuses, condemns, and executes Bigger even before he has been caught and tried for the murder. Added to this horror is the frenzied hostility and hatred within the white community surrounding the Black Belt. The mounting hatred intensifies Bigger's terror as the police move closer and closer to their prey. We are reminded of the rat Bigger chased. Now white society is trying to trap Bigger like a rat so they can reduce him once again to the status of a "nigger." Crouching behind one object after another, Bigger becomes trapped in a maze of old buildings. This is his world, the cramped environment that has kept him captive all his life. It is the world that has kept him shut out from all thought and feeling, will and mind, aspiration and satisfaction. Fear replaces fatigue as he scurries from one cold building to another cold building, seeking refuge, knowing that there is really no safe place now to go.

Bigger's hunger for life, his long struggle to survive, is evident throughout this scene as Bigger attempts to escape white society and its laws. He knows by instinct, as all blacks know by instinct, that the white man's laws dispose of blacks, guilty or not, one way or another. He knows too that he has no other place to turn except back to that same black ghetto from which he has all his life tried to escape. He realizes that his only chance for survival — if he is to survive at all — is to hide among the remnants of his past life.

Starting from the place where he killed Bessie — somewhere near 50th Street — Bigger steadily moves from apartment to apartment until he reaches 53rd Street. Closing his eyes and clutching a stolen newspaper, he mentally calculates the position of the police as he visualizes the shaded portions already covered in last night's raids on black homes. It should be noted that these same homes were once inhabited by rich whites, but long ago they abandoned them for better housing on the other side of town, leaving them for blacks to live in, daring blacks to move out of the shaded areas. Thus the Black Belt to which Bigger returns is really Bigger himself. It contains Bigger's entire life. It is part of Bigger Thomas' psyche. It literally, and at the same time, figuratively, represents the realities of life, the emptiness of his entire existence.

Like the constant beating of the drums in O'Neill's drama *The Emperor Jones,* the steady pursuit of the white lawmen has a profound psychological effect on Bigger's mind as the chase closes in. Wandering around the rooftop of the building on 53rd Street, he is soon discovered and slowly he begins to lose his chance for survival; that is, flight. Once he was a new, "big" man; now he reverts to being black, a scared little boy in a brutal white world. At the end of Book II his resemblance to the Bigger Thomas before the two murders is remarkable. He is once more a "nigger." As his head bumps first down one flight of steps, then down another, he closes his eyes and tries to shut out the world. He tried to rise out of the black world where the white man kept him down. And he did; to himself, he gained new stature, and just before he is captured he is, literally, above the white men, but he is brought savagely down and he is, again, literally, dragged down, step by step, back to the black world, and into a new, confined ghetto: prison.

BOOK III
FATE

Bigger has been caught and imprisoned, and even though he is as good as dead in the white man's world, he is still, nevertheless, very much physically alive. His destruction is not accomplished until the end of Book III. Before that time, Bigger himself must be able to realize, at least partially, some of his own failures for which hitherto he has blamed society. At the same time, the reader must also be aware of certain concepts about Bigger's psyche perhaps not quite so thoroughly discussed up to now.

Wright therefore allows Bigger to face some of the realities of life but, at the same time, does not destroy all of Bigger's concepts about the evils of racism and its effects upon the black experience. To accomplish this, Wright devotes many pages of dialogue to the black-white dilemma; he introduces Max, a white Communist lawyer, into the plot to talk to Bigger. At this point, the action slows to a standstill as we listen to a sort of civil rights plea from Wright himself (as the lawyer). It is a plea to the white society in America during the 30s that had pressed and imprisoned the black society into a hostile knot of fear and frustration. As such, it operates on two levels. It serves to show how whites shaped black Bigger. It also shows how Max and the Communist party were unable to accept Bigger as a person, as a human. To them, Bigger was only an object shaped by a capitalistic white society. In truth, however, both societies have no place for a black Bigger. It is not a thoroughly humanistic appeal that Max makes; it is also a sociological appeal, in many ways no different from that offered by the Daltons.

Bigger is thrown into jail to await his fate, a fate which he realizes all too well is already sealed, but Bigger's fate was sealed long before he was born: he was born black in a white-ruled society. He therefore sinks again behind his blank wall of illusion, his refuge. For three days he lies in a mental stupor, refusing to acknowledge anything. Having been forced all his life into a world of false estimates, false stereotypes, and false relationships, Bigger senses that his total impressions of that world will never be correct. He lies stagnant; to him, the sum total of his life is failure, failure even after he has murdered twice in order to find some kind of order and meaning to his life. Having killed twice in order to purge his soul of conflicts and issues brought on by inherent fears, he desires now to blot out himself and his whole existence.

However, when Bigger is confronted with the white crowd, his will to live springs up. This is typical of Wright's protagonists; they always accept the challenge thrown at them. Big Boy, in the short story "Big Boy Leaves Home," is told not to get his clothes. A white woman stands on them, daring him to come forward; but, even though he is urged by other black kids to stay back, Big Boy does claim his clothes and thus his dignity. Bigger, like Big Boy, senses that the white crowd wants him to blot out his existence so that they can have a better sport of his death. With this realization, Bigger's will to live comes back to him.

It is through Bigger's struggle with his will to live that Wright leads us to the many purposes of this section of the novel, "Fate." As soon as Bigger killed Mary, his outcome was known; in fact, it was known as soon as he was born. White society asked him to accept his living conditions, to be content with the realities of black life or he would end up on the gallows, as he is warned by his mother. "Fate" also represents the kind of defense Max will offer for Bigger; he is a product of his environment, hence a native son. Yet "Fate" also suggests that Bigger is fated to realize for the first time who he is; that is, he must understand his own actions and take responsibility for them.

As Bigger regains consciousness, he realizes how terribly alone he is. Life is a farce, a joke played on him by a cruel and unjust God, a God in whom he must not believe, for to believe in God would be emotional suicide. So believe he must not. Therefore, when Bigger is visited in his cell by the black minister, the Daltons, and Bigger's own family, they all become a mass of meaningless humanity with which he cannot identify. His previous convictions of becoming a unique being with vital and deep meanings are gone. He turns his face from everything and everybody. He does not wish to become a part of his mother's religion or her faith in God. He refuses the spiritual blessings offered him by the black minister. He has no desire to sustain himself. The facts of his failure are known; he has been caught and he must die for his failures. He is again locked behind a wall, but this time it is the white man's physical wall, solid stone and secure — in addition to his own wall of fear and confusion.

In allowing Bigger to reveal how he feels about his situation, and about life in general, to Max, his lawyer, Wright uses his hero as a mouthpiece so that the reader can better understand the racial crisis. Today's reader might wonder about the author's use of Max, a Communist, to defend his hero, Bigger Thomas, but he should realize, first of all, that Bigger himself is not a Communist; neither does he know the tenets of communism. However, one must keep in mind the fact that Richard Wright was once an active member of the Communist party and saw a great value in the party's relationship to the black revolution for equal justice under the law.

In the 1930s, the American Communist party was the only white political body that promised hope for the black man. It campaigned among the Negroes on the basis of the Negroes' right to national self-determination in the southern parts of the United States. Also, many of their workers hammered away at the Negroes in the tightly-packed segregated areas of the North as well. The Communist appeal came at a time when blacks in lid-tight ghetto belts of blight cities like Chicago, Detroit, and New York were beginning to want and demand their rights to equal jobs and equal opportunities, to equal education and to equal places in white America. Max and Jan are not Communists, then, so much as they are men who are interested in people, and who also happen to be active Communists, and who come to Bigger's defense. There were just such men in the 30s. We may not agree with Wright's choice of defender, but this humanistic, political appeal to Negroes was very strongly felt in Chicago's Black Belt where there was little else left to hope for.

When Bigger forces his mind to think again, he realizes the utter futility of ever escaping the electric chair; he sits and waits in his jail cell for his ultimate fate. Max struggles with the district attorney to see that Bigger gets a fair trial, but Bigger knows his situation. He knows, for example, that the only evidence really needed to convict him of murder is the evidence discovered in Mary's death. He knows further that Bessie's death really does not matter at all to "them." It is Mary's death that matters because Mary was white. Had Bigger murdered only Bessie, the white police could have cared less. To them, it would have meant "just another dead nigger."

Here again the author's deep psychological descriptions of Bigger's inner conflicts arising out of fear and antagonism for white racism closely parallels Dostoevsky's description of Raskolnikov's inner conflicts concerning his place in the universe. Both heroes, or anti-heroes, as the case may be, feel strangely rooted in an evil which they themselves can hardly explain. Raskolnikov attributes his downfall to fate; Bigger, to white racism. In reflecting upon his own situation, Bigger can trace the pattern of his existence and the existence of his whole life back to white racism. Forced into a racial system of checks and balances, he notes that he was "their" property, heart and soul, body and blood; what they did claimed every atom of him, sleeping and waking. He was made to live one place, while they lived another. He had no choice — ever. And for one reason: he was black.

Such conditions, Wright says, breed the Bigger Thomases of the world. There are no provisions made for individual differences, for human dignity and self-confidence. Again and again the author underscores the age-old problem of man's inhumanity to man and attributes these forces of evil to white racist hatred and economic and social injustices within the American political structure. Through the pressures and complexities of living in the Black Belt, Bigger—before he murdered a white girl—was figuratively murdered by the white man. They denied him life, but he managed to exist. Now they are preparing to end his life absolutely.

Bigger Thomas foreshadows the new black man of today; that is, he is a black man who re-creates himself in *his* own image rather than allow the white man to do so. In order to believe in himself, he—not the white man—is the creator. Bigger tells Max that what he killed for, that's what he is.

Although Max is used, because he is a lawyer, to verbalize Wright's warning to white society, the reader should realize that when Bigger defends himself, when he states that killing Mary was good because it allowed him to begin to come to terms with the hate and fear stored inside of him, Max cannot understand. He is so shocked at what Bigger is saying that he cannot even touch Bigger.

The first jail scene allows Wright to bring together all the people who have affected Bigger's life. The implied question here is: who is to share the responsibility with Bigger? The Daltons, who create the ghettos, wash their hands of responsibility by giving away ping-pong tables. The black church says that life, thus black life, is one of suffering. Mrs. Thomas, who has never really tried to understand her son, is she to share some of the blame? It is only Jan who begins to see that Bigger has no reason for viewing him as being any different from the whites who are calling for his life. Jan is willing to share some of the blame. Jan is no longer as blind as he was in Book I. He serves as a foil to Max, who has understood Bigger only in a sociological sense, never as an individual.

Bigger had thought Max was his friend, that his defense in court showed that Max understood how Bigger felt. In the final jail scene, Bigger, who is non-articulate, struggles to tell Max how he feels. It is here that Bigger knows that Max is only trying to comfort him in the face of death; thus he sends Max away. As Max walks out of the cell, he is described as a blind man. Notice it is here that Bigger refers to Jan not as Mr. Erlone but with the first name, emphasizing the contrast with Max.

It becomes apparent at the beginning of the trial that the black man has never been a free agent in the American structure. He has never been able to arrange his own life according to his own wishes and desires. The white structure has always placed him—the black man—in a regulated pattern. Even in the most personal areas of his life, the black man has been told what to think and what to do by the white power structure. His only comfort has been in sex, whiskey, and religion. How does one escape from crowded, rat-infested tenements with no future? Sex, whiskey, and religion help; and then there are other ways that a black man can lash out, violently, at his black world and at the white world for being partners in the master-slave society in America: he can rob, rape, and murder.

Unfortunately, as Max emphasizes, when the black man chooses to rebel, very often he is *forced* to commit murder. Max appeals, therefore, to some inner consciousness of decency within the whites themselves who *must* feel obligated to begin to alleviate this dangerously explosive situation. And here Wright becomes a master of rhetoric; note that it is filled with imagery and symbolism in order to color the despair of Bigger's world and the world of all blacks living under the heel of the white man. However, the issue involved is much larger than merely the death of one black man. Much more important is the issue of the black-white relationship in American society. When this relationship fosters murder, and continues to foster murder, then surely something drastic will surely happen to the whole structural body itself. Wright accurately predicts much of the racial violence that rocked this nation in the late 60s.

Confronted then with the very difficult task of not really saving Bigger's life but of preventing other Biggers from developing and fermenting, the author pleads, *begs*, the white society to listen, to allow the black man freedom of movement, the same freedom the white man has. This, in part, explains Max's urgent plea for Bigger's life: if a component of the whole continues to be oppressed, not only will that small component become rotten, but it will become like a cancer and attack the entire body — until that body is destroyed.

At the end of the novel Bigger is an existential man, a theme Wright is later to develop in his novel, *The Outsider*. Bigger is alone, yet able to comfort himself in the face of death because he takes the individual's responsibility of being what he is. White society was demanding him to be submissive, to be content with the rat-infested housing, with relief, to be thankful for being lucky enough to drive a white man's car. Bigger was expected to live with fear and self-hatred. To be himself, to be a man meant that he had to take pride in killing Mary. He had to kill Bessie not only to continue to survive but also because he had accepted himself as a murderer. The white world allowed Bigger only one way to have responsibility over himself. Notice also that the only character who comes close to understanding Bigger is Jan, whose last name is Er*lone*. Bigger has grown from no man in the beginning of the novel to something bigger than man at the end of the novel. He must die in the electric chair for his crime against society, but it is not the author's intention to obstruct justice for the sake of a principle. Sentence is passed and Bigger must die, but Wright has had his way in a warning to the white world: it is not the Biggers who will ultimately burn; it is the white world. Learn or burn!

CHARACTER ANALYSES

BIGGER THOMAS

The dramatic conflict of *Native Son* takes place chiefly within the mind of its leading character, Bigger Thomas, who lives in a world of illusions and dreams. To Bigger, all of life is conflict, surrounded by a White Wall that keeps him on the "outside peeping in through a knothole in the fence." The reader is aware from the beginning of the novel that Bigger is waging a war between himself and the outside white world.

Before the murder of Mary Dalton, Bigger's self-concept was governed by the white man. The white man gave Bigger a feeling of self-inadequacy, a feeling of incompleteness, and an urge for self-destruction. After the murder, however, Bigger Thomas becomes "big" to himself. His mind confuses the accidental death of Mary Dalton with a conscious desire to kill all white women who have left him in a world of self-debasement. He views his act as an act of the will. He feels now that he is no longer "conditioned" by what white people want him to feel. He thereby re-creates his own image and becomes his own god. Bigger has power; he is Somebody. He is an embodiment of the black revolt against the injustices of the white caste society. By accident, and for a while, Bigger is free of the white man's yoke. He stretches, he flexes his manhood, and revolts. And his revolt takes the form of violence and revenge against white society.

In the section entitled "How 'Bigger' Was Born," the author discusses several kinds of "Biggers" whom he met while growing up. Wright asserts that it is from his association and his relationship with these various Biggers that he drew his character of Bigger Thomas. Out of the Biggers that Wright knew during his first twenty years in the South, he chooses five specific types to represent the total concept of his character in *Native Son*. In describing each type of Bigger, Wright narrates an incident from his own experience. For example, Bigger No. 1 is brutal; he reminds the reader of the Bigger who brutalizes Gus in Doc's poolroom. Bigger No. 2 constantly complains; this type suggests Bigger and his hoodlum friends who say over and over that "white folks got everything and we got nothing." Bigger No. 3 is the type who walks into movie theaters without paying and dares the black ticket taker to object. Bigger No. 4 reminds the reader more and more of the hero in this novel, the Bigger whose warped mind cannot discern illusion from reality. Bigger No. 5 is a little braver than our hero; he openly defies the Jim Crow laws of the South and objects vehemently to being an "outsider."

Wright chooses these five types as composite Biggers. In describing each type he has known, Wright points out to the reader that, psychologically, Bigger Thomas has already become an "outsider," even as the novel opens. This Bigger Thomas is hostile to everyone, even to his own people.

Wright feels that all Biggers, however, are the products of American civilization and are thereby "native sons." It is American society, with its Jim Crow laws and its debasement of the black man, that has created all of the Bigger Thomases of America. They are America's real native sons.

It is important that the reader observes that each type of Bigger revolts against the conduct established for him by prejudiced white America. For instance, during the period of time that the novel takes place, Negroes in both the South and the North were considered inherently inferior to whites, both mentally and physically. It was expected that since "niggers" were not really human, they should be isolated from the rest of American society. When Bigger revolts, the whites do not see a human being struggling for human dignity and recognition; rather, they see what they ignorantly choose to see: a dangerous beast, escaped from the ghetto.

Yet Bigger Thomas *is* a man. This is Wright's thesis – to show us a portrait of a man and the reason he revolts. Besides being a man, Bigger Thomas is also every black man who no longer identifies with either his own people and their modes of living, their religion, their culture, or with the white society and its mode of living. Bigger Thomas is any black man who cannot be conditioned by the white man's laws, rules and regulations that place his life in a vortex of no meaning. In addition, Bigger Thomas is all men – black or white – whose lives have lost real meaning, real experience. Not all Bigger Thomases are black men locked in the Black Belts of Chicago or New York or any other big American city, waiting to rape or to kill white women. Regardless of their race, creed or national origin, the Bigger Thomases of this world cannot and will not accept oppression.

MRS. THOMAS

Mrs. Thomas provides us with a background for Bigger's actions. She has no interest in civil rights nor any understanding of the masculine frustration within Bigger. She has given up fighting for self-respect from the white man, if indeed she ever thought about it. She simply wants Bigger to get a "nigger-type" job and be a good boy. She recognizes that Bigger has a wild streak in him and forecasts some of the ill-fated things that are going to happen to him. She warns him that "You'll regret how you living some day." And, in this sense, she is like mothers everywhere who want their boys to stay out of trouble and be happy.

In Book III, Mrs. Thomas comes with Vera and Buddy to Bigger's cell. Being poor and old and tired, she finds it hard to understand the circumstances of Bigger's crime or his arrest. She begs the Daltons for his life and cries to the court for mercy. In her ardent appeal for her son's life, she turns to God, to the church, and to her belief in the forgiveness of sin as her sole consolation. She has little hope of the black man ever receiving justice from the white man; religion is her solace, her escape from reality.

VERA THOMAS

Perhaps one of the most minor characters in the novel is Vera, Bigger's sister. Mentioned first in the bedroom scene, where Bigger kills the rat and dangles it before her eyes, Vera succumbs to fear and faints. This method of introducing Vera signifies the whole of Vera's existence: fear. She lives continuously with fear; in fact, her fear is so great that Wright tells us that she often seems to be "shrinking from life in every gesture" she makes. Even the way she sits shows a fear so deep as to be an organic part of her. She fears the world, she fears herself, her family, and certainly the white man. She never knows when a blow is going to strike. And this is not "simple" animal fear; this is a human being's fear. Animals do not know that they are afraid; they simply react. Vera is afraid, is aware of her fear, so must live not only within the black ghetto but also within the confines of constant fear.

Vera appears three times in the novel as an extension of Bigger's family background; her character is really never developed to any degree, but she is an extension of Bigger's fear and the fear that any black person feels in an environment festering with hatred and frustration. Vera is not strong enough to fight the white menace; she is too frightened, even of Bigger, to defy the edicts of racism. Vera is synonymous with victim, one of many.

BUDDY THOMAS

Like his sister Vera, Buddy is an extension of Bigger. Like Bigger, Buddy was born into the black world, a world filled with shame, fear, and frustration. But, unlike Bigger who rebels against this world, Buddy accepts the subservient role assigned to him by the white caste society. He is willing to play the humble "nigger" who knows his place and keeps in his place. In Wright's autobiography, *Black Boy*, he depicts many kinds of Buddys who, in their struggle to live, blot from their minds all rebellion and meekly accept the double standards of inequality.

Buddy is decidedly different from Bigger. He admires his big brother even though he does not try to copy his actions. Bigger continually refers to both his brother and his sister as being blind to the real things that matter in life. Bigger neither loves nor pities them; he merely tolerates their being a part of his world. Bigger is not willing to live a Jim Crow existence once he has broken the white man's bonds. Buddy, however, has no such challenge; he is willing to live on the white man's terms, rather than make the terms himself.

MARY DALTON

Mary Dalton, the young, vivacious, and beautiful heiress to the Dalton fortune, irritates and overwhelms Bigger Thomas with her friendliness. She is indeed an embodiment of all sorts of white women whom he has tried to avoid all his life, knowing deeply within himself that being involved with a white woman, no matter what the circumstances are, is ultimate death to a black man. Her inquiries about his personal life and about whether or not he belongs to a union (she equates unions with communism) confuse him. He hates Mary Dalton and wants to blot her from his mind. However, he knows that this is impossible since it is she whom he has to chauffeur around the city. But a sixth sense, an uncanny warning resounding somewhere deeply within the psyche of all black men, warns him that Mary Dalton means trouble for him and, more particularly, death. To Bigger, Mary Dalton's very presence is a threat to his security—and his life.

When Mary announces to Bigger a few blocks from her home that she does not intend to go to the university, but rather that she intends to meet a friend, this news is startling to an already bewildered young black man. Laughingly, she tries to put Bigger's troubled mind at ease by explaining that Jan is a special friend to Bigger, as well as to her, and that he is a Communist whose main object in life is to help "colored people" gain equal rights with whites.

It is apparent to the reader that Mary Dalton is a white bourgeois who considers the black man a person, but a different kind of person. For instance, she tells Bigger that Negroes must live somewhat as whites live because, after all, "they are *human.*" What she means is that they are supposed to be human; so, as a matter of course, they should live like *white* folks. She is a shallow girl, and Bigger tries to shun her as much as possible, but when the threat of his own safety becomes a reality, he acts in the only way open to him: he kills Mary Dalton and all the other Mary Daltons who have ever threatened or challenged his right to exist.

JAN ERLONE

Jan's role in the novel is at first much the same as Mary Dalton's role, the only difference being in sex. Just as white women have always brought a certain kind of threat to the black man in American society, so have white men. It is soon discerned by the reader that although Jan Erlone and Mary Dalton seriously consider themselves friends to the black and the oppressed, they are using Bigger as a pawn in their game of communism.

Jan's apparent display of friendship is not accepted kindly by Bigger who has never before shaken a white man's hand. He becomes afraid and frustrated as Jan's extended hand symbolizes the threat of white oppression. To Bigger, an extended white hand carries a rope, a gun, or both; we recall that Bigger's father was killed in the South for racial reasons. Bigger shrinks from Jan's handshake and becomes bottled up with pain when Jan insists upon being called by his first name. Jan Erlone is a white man, one of the enemy; Bigger can fathom nothing else.

Basically, this is the reason Bigger finds it so easy to blame the murder of Mary Dalton upon the white frame of Jan Erlone, a fact which Jan in all sincerity cannot understand. Again, when Bigger points his gun at Jan, Jan is shocked with disbelief; he cannot understand Bigger's hostility because he himself has always tried to be friendly to Bigger. But, of course, Jan did not grow up with a psychological gun at his head, held by a black man.

At the end of the novel, one should note that because Jan is able to understand his blame in the crime and in the way Bigger was forced to live, Bigger does become, in a sense, "friends" with Jan.

MAX

The author's use of a Marxist Communist to defend his hero, Bigger Thomas, is understandable in view of the fact that at the time this novel was being written (1938-40), Richard Wright, along with other well-known American and European writers and painters, was an active member of the Communist party. However, nowhere in the novel does Max try to persuade Bigger to embrace the tenets of communism. He knows too well that Bigger's mind cannot grasp the social basis for communism in America. He does try and explain, though, that he himself, as a Communist lawyer, has taken the case because he knows that other white Americans would not be willing to defend a black man for murdering a white girl.

Max's Communistic beliefs embrace all mistreated and misguided minority peoples everywhere. Wright's deep philosophical descriptions of the motives of communism are uttered through Max's defense of Bigger in order to appease the left-wingers of his own party. Wright knew that most of the party members would be displeased with his concept of Bigger's plight in American society. Therefore, he uses Max as Bigger's "guardian angel." In using Max as the defense lawyer, Wright hoped to mellow the party's displeasure against himself and against his hero, Bigger Thomas. Yet Wright, making Max as blind as the others, was bound to upset members of the party. Wright was willing to show that Communists viewed the Negro as a sociological statistic to be used as one of the party's political tools.

BUCKLEY

Chicago's white — and brutal — prosecuting attorney could not have been better named or depicted to drive home the lesson that every black man in America should learn: the white man's inhumanity to the black man. The name *Buckley* carries the connotations of *butt, batter,* and *bash.* It is synonymous with a sawhorse, a male animal, and with the verbs, *bolster, bear, upbear, brace, straddle,* and *sustain.* These things, naturally, mean very little in isolation, but when one studies the character of Buckley, we realize that his sole function is to butt, batter, and bash in the head, heart, and soul of a black man who has unwittingly killed a white girl. Thus the symbolism carries a keen and heavy meaning.

Buckley is merciless in his presentation of the case against Bigger. To him, as to all other whites in the novel (with the

exception of Jan and Max), Bigger Thomas is guilty even before
he is tried. No one dares entertain the notion of "accidental murder." Rape is immediately associated with the murder; in addition, Buckley tries desperately to indict Bigger for other crimes —
a point which Wright also makes in his autobiography, *Black
Boy:* when a Negro is caught for a crime, it is understood that he
is probably guilty of many more unsolved crimes.

Buckley is out to get Bigger Thomas and he does. And Max's
humane appeal seems almost ridiculous, at times, in light of
Buckley's prejudice against all black men in America.

BRITTEN

Hired as Mr. Dalton's own private detective, Britten is the
first link that connects Bigger with the facts of the crime. He
correlates the action of the crime by being present when Bigger
returns to the Dalton house and by participating in Bigger's in-
quisition. He is also present when the reporters accidentally
discover the evidence in the ashes of the furnace.

Though typically white and prejudiced against the black
man from the ghetto, Britten is not as vicious as his counterpart,
the prosecuting attorney. Britten sets the stage for the court trial
and prepares the reader for the worst. His questions to Bigger
concerning the actions of Mary Dalton anticipate the questions
Buckley will ask.

In one sense, Britten serves as a link between the reader and
past events. He reviews the events leading up to the murder,
thus allowing the reader to anticipate Bigger's responses. Britten himself is not smart enough to believe that Bigger is the murderer; on the other hand, he does not think that Bigger is smart
enough to kill a rich white heiress and then to send a ransom
note, demanding ten thousand dollars for her return. Either
way, Britten never traps Bigger in the interim between the
murder and the capture.

MR. DALTON

As one of the major characters, Mr. Dalton's role is exclusively that of the System, that looming white mountain that stands between Bigger Thomas and the world of reality. Mr. Dalton, father to Mary Dalton, and the rich white owner of many tenement houses in the Black Belt of Chicago, contributes huge sums of money to black recreational centers and to the NAACP, a feat which neither impresses nor improves Bigger Thomas' attitude toward the white power structure. Bigger cares nothing at all for the Daltons; he considers their acts of charity as acts of hostility. The black cause is not alleviated by baseballs and footballs and pool tables. The black cause is pain and hunger and humiliation and fear and frustration surrounded by white indifference. Bigger's hatred for the Daltons of this world is second only to his hatred of himself. It is people like Mr. Dalton who are the Judas Iscariots of this world: they shake your hand and cut your throat at the same time.

MRS. DALTON

Although physically blind, Mrs. Dalton is cast in a very peculiar role. In most works of literature, physically blind characters often have uncanny psychological insight: Oedipus Rex, for instance, is physically blind but he is able to fathom more of reality because of this handicap. But Mrs. Dalton is no wiser for her blindness. She typifies the average American white woman who is totally ignorant about the black experience. She, like most white women, never even tries to imagine what it must be like to live four people to a room — and share it with rats. She tries to do her bit for the "poor" by giving them games.

Like her husband, Mrs. Dalton is a part of the white establishment that helps to keep alive the fires of racial hatred. For instance, she cannot *possibly* conceive of Bigger's presence in her daughter's bedroom at two o'clock in the morning. If a white man were there taking care of Mary, putting her to bed, Mrs.

Dalton would be surprised, but not thunderstruck, as she would be if she knew Bigger were there. In her private white world, Mrs. Dalton has reared her only child. And, like Mrs. Thomas, Mrs. Dalton cannot understand some of her child's ways, but Mrs. Dalton does not worry too terribly about Mary because Mary is rich and well brought up and white.

BESSIE

Basic love is absent from Bigger's affair with Bessie. Sex and lust are the motivating forces that drive Bigger to Bessie. Escapism drives Bessie to Bigger. Bessie works long hours in the hot kitchen of a white family six days a week and finds no better, or other, outlet for her frustrations and fears than whiskey and Bigger. Even though she does not love Bigger, she tolerates him, mainly because he buys her cheap whiskey.

Like Bigger, Bessie believes in nothing, not even in herself; however, unlike Bigger, thought never penetrates the walls of her unconscious mind. She moves about automatically, like a robot driven only by such needs as food, clothing, and shelter. Sex in itself means nothing to her. It is only a means of being able to get drinks for which she does not have to pay. As a matter of course, she aids Bigger in stealing small articles from the whites for whom she works. In terms of the naturalistic situation, Bessie's plight cannot be explained; thought is simply not part of her psyche. She does not struggle, not even when Bigger forces her to become a part of a murder about which she knows nothing. Her weak protestations are not actual struggles.

Bessie's murder is an expression of Bigger's self-hate and his inability to love. He is able to kill her immediately after he has made love to her. Her murder also makes sure that the reader sees Bigger as a murderer. In addition, it serves to show how "justice" values Mary's life more than Bessie's.

JACK, G. H., and GUS

These three minor characters are hoodlum friends of Bigger. They do nothing to control the events of the plot; they serve merely as a kind of backdrop to Bigger's environmental struggle to overcome the bleak world of illusion. They rob the black community because they are afraid to venture into the surrounding white community.

There are three meetings among the boys. The first meeting concerns their plans to rob Blum's store. The second meeting takes place in Doc's after Bigger has murdered Mary Dalton. Since most of Bigger's fears and tensions have left him after he has murdered Mary, he treats the three boys to cigarettes and acts "biggerty." This act both shocks and amazes the boys. The third meeting occurs in Bigger's jail cell. Again, the boys serve only to emphasize the role which Bigger plays in the novel. They are definitely not foils, but they do serve to strengthen the background of the hero.

One should note that rather than take the leading role in staging and executing the robbery, Gus *allows* Bigger to beat him up; thus, the reader not only sees, but feels Gus's cowardice. Even though Gus does not threaten Bigger, Gus does permit Bigger to humiliate him in front of his friends rather than force the real issue: robbing a white man's store.

About G. H., the second member of the gang, nothing much need be said. He moves in realms of shadows and serves only as a member of the gang. The few irrelevant questions which he asks Bigger from time to time are of little importance. The reader might note that G. H. has no given name, just G. H., a point which signifies a sort of non-existence within the action of the novel.

Jack, although not the stated leader or the implied leader of the gang, takes on the role of appeaser or pacificist. Apparently, Bigger likes him or rather respects him. He neither bullies nor threatens Jack. They go to the movies together and talk about the black-white problem. When the fight starts between Gus and Bigger, Jack tries to arbitrate the issue, though not very emphatically. He cautions Bigger not to kill Gus, but no one steps in the path of Bigger's wrath.

PEGGY

Although Peggy, the housekeeper, might be considered a minor character, she serves a very vital role in the construction of the development of the plot. After all, it is Peggy who admits Bigger into the Dalton household, who introduces him to his chores, and who tells him the secrets of the family's success. By no means, then, is Peggy minor; however, in another sense, that of altering the physical or emotional status of Bigger's life, which has already been shaped and sharpened by years of privation, prejudice, and bitterness, she does nothing.

It should be noted that Peggy has served the Daltons for many years and has become one of the family, so to speak. She knows, for instance, how the Daltons feel about Negroes. She reveals to Bigger that Mrs. Dalton has often encouraged her husband to contribute huge sums of money to black recreational centers and has even helped a few blacks to better themselves by attending night school. She tells Bigger how Mrs. Dalton helped Green, the last black chauffeur, to go to night school, thus permitting him to get a better job with the government. But Peggy feels superior to Bigger; she is white and he is black, and even though she seems kind, she is nonetheless patronizing.

REVIEW QUESTIONS

1. In Book I, why does Bigger always feel "hot" inside and "uptight" about his life in general?

2. Explain his attitude toward his mother, his sister, and his brother. Why is he always so hostile toward them?

3. Why is Bigger so brutal to Gus? Be specific.

4. In what ways does Gus serve as a scapegoat to Bigger's frustrations and disappointments in life?

5. Why does Bigger deliberately slice Doc's pool table cloth?

6. What specific purpose does this act serve?

7. Discuss the significance of the images of color, sound, and sight to the action of Book I.

8. Find at least four concrete examples of irony in Book I. Explain the use of each example in its relation to the action of Book I.

9. When Bigger finds himself alone in Mary's bedroom with her blind mother coming into the room, why does he not simply explain the situation to Mary's mother instead of smothering Mary to death? Explain.

10. What major purposes does the clock serve throughout Book I?

11. At the end of Book I, why does Bigger go home to sleep?

12. What symbolic purpose does cutting off Mary's head serve in the action of the plot?

13. What alibi does Bigger plan to use and why?

14. Why doesn't Bigger like Jan Erlone?

15. At the beginning of Book II, why do Bigger's eyes "pop" suddenly open?

16. Of what significance is the imagery of "snow" and "cold" at the beginning of Book II?

17. Why does Bigger feel that his whole family is "suddenly blind"? that Mary, too, was "blind"? that Jan was "blind"? that even the Daltons are "blind"? Interrelate the "blind" theory throughout Books I and II.

18. If Mrs. Dalton is actually blind, why does Bigger include her also?

19. In Book I, when Bigger steps into the Dalton kitchen to get a drink of water (before Mary's death), he senses that blind Mrs. Dalton knows that he is there. He senses that most blind people develop an uncanny power to "feel" one's presence. Why then does Mrs. Dalton not sense that Bigger Thomas is in the room with her daughter on the night of the murder?

20. Discuss the irony of this situation: Mr. Dalton owns the rat-infested tenement house in which Bigger Thomas lives crowded with his family; later, Bigger laments the fact that "they live there and we live here" and kills Mary, their daughter.

21. Discuss Bigger's meaning in the following statements:
The black girl was merely "evidence."
What his mother had was Bessie's whiskey, and Bessie's whiskey was his mother's religion.
White people never searched for Negroes who killed other Negroes.

22. Outline Bigger's strategic plan to escape detection and, at the same time, to collect the ransom money.

23. Why doesn't his plan work?

24. What role does Bigger's girl friend, Bessie, play in his plans? (not her role as his sex partner)

25. Why does Bigger finally kill Bessie?

26. What part does Bessie's death play in the main action of the plot? Explain and give specific references.

27. Why do the Negroes of Chicago live in the Black Belt, a "small, shaded" portion of the city? Why don't they move around as "free" agents?

28. Relate the newspaper accounts of Bigger's crime to present-day accounts of crimes committed by Negroes. Go to your public library to search the files for such accounts.

29. Specifically, what does each newspaper account tell you about the people of that day in Chicago or elsewhere in the nation?

30. Was the North any different from the South in its treatment of the Negro? Seek outside sources if you do not have first-hand information.

31. How did the police officials in this novel treat Bigger? Give specific examples.

32. What is the author, as a kind of central intelligence, saying to the reader? Why?

33. Why and how is Bigger finally caught at the end of Book II?

34. Trace specific references as to how Bigger feels about himself. Why?

35. How do his feelings about himself influence the action of his life? Explain.

36. Why does Wright choose Max, a Communist lawyer, to defend his hero, Bigger Thomas?

37. Why is it that Max's defense of Bigger, though eloquent and rhetorical, does not save Bigger's life? That is, why *must* Bigger die in the electric chair for his crime?

38. Do you think that Bigger should have gotten the chair? Why or why not? Be concrete. Give direct reasons supported by evidence.

39. Had Bigger lived during the 1960s or thereafter, would he have gotten the chair? Be specific.

SELECTED BIBLIOGRAPHY

ALGREN, N. "Remembering Richard Wright." *Nation* (January, 1961), 85-87.

BALDWIN, JAMES. "The Survival of Richard Wright." *Nation*, (March, 1961), 52-53.

BASSO, HAMILTON. "Thomas Jefferson and the Black Boy." *New Yorker*, XXI (March 10, 1945), 86.

BONE, ROBERT A. *The Negro Novel in America.* New Haven: Yale University Press, 1958.

BROWN, STERLING A. "Criticism of Richard Wright." *Nation* (April, 1938), 448.

BURGAN, EDWARD B. *The Art of Richard Wright's Short Stories.* New York: Oxford University Press, 1947.

CAIN, ALFRED E., *et al. The Negro Heritage Library.* New York: Educational Heritage Incorporated, 1968.

ELLISON, RALPH. "Richard Wright's Blues." *The Antioch Review Anthology*, ed., PAUL BIXLER. New York: World Publishing Co., 1953.

ESTES, RICE. "Freedom to Read." *Library Journal*, LIV (December 15, 1960), 4421-22.

HARRINGTON, OLLIE. "The Last Days of Richard Wright." *Ebony*, LXXVII (February, 1969), 83-86.

HICKS, GRANVILLE. "The Power of Richard Wright." *Saturday Review*, XX (October 18, 1958), 65.

HOWE, IRVING. "Richard Wright: A Word of Farewell." *The New Republic* (February, 1961), 17-18.

CARL MILTON HUGHES. *The Negro Novelist (1940-50)*. New York: Citadel Press, 1953.

JONES, H. M. "Up from Slavery: Richard Wright's Story." *Saturday Review of Literature*, XXVIII (March 3, 1945), 9.

KENNEDY, RAYMOND. "A Dramatic Autobiography." *Yale Review*, XXXIV (Summer, 1945), 762.

KUNTZ, R. *Twentieth Century Authors*. New York: H. W. Wilson Co., 1955.

MARGOLIES, EDWARD. *The Art of Richard Wright*. Carbondale: Southern Illinois University Press, 1969.

MCCALL, DAN. *The Example of Richard Wright*. New York: Harcourt, Brace and World, Inc., 1969.

PRESCOTT, ORVILLE. *In My Opinion*. New York: Bobbs-Merrill Company, Inc., 1932.

PLOSKI, HARRY A., and ROSCOE BROWN. "Richard Wright." *The Negro Almanac*, II (1968), 49-50.

WEBB, CONSTANCE. *Richard Wright: A Biography*. New York: G. P. Putnam's Sons, 1968.

WHITE, RALPH K. "*Black Boy*: A Value Analysis." *Journal of Abnormal Psychology*, XLIII (October, 1947), 44.

NOTES

NOTES